C000184192

Exploring British Values

Individual Liberty

Catherine Chambers

a Capstone company — publishers for children

Raintree is an imprint of Capstone Global Library Limited, a company incorporated in England and Wales having its registered office at 264 Banbury Road, Oxford, OX2 7DY – Registered company number: 6695582

www.raintree.co.uk
myorders@raintree.co.uk

Text © Capstone Global Library Limited 2018

The moral rights of the proprietor have been asserted.

All rights reserved. No part of this publication may be reproduced in any form or by any means (including photocopying or storing it in any medium by electronic means and whether or not transiently or incidentally to some other use of this publication) without the written permission of the copyright owner, except in accordance with the provisions of the Copyright, Designs and Patents Act 1988 or under the terms of a licence issued by the Copyright Licensing Agency, Saffron House, 6–10 Kirby Street, London EC1N 8TS (www.cla.co.uk). Applications for the copyright owner's written permission should be addressed to the publisher.

Edited by Linda Staniford
Designed by Terri Poburka
Picture research by Pam Mitsakos
Original illustrations © Capstone Global Library Limited 2018
Illustrated by Graham Ross
Production by Steve Walker
Originated by Capstone Global Library
Printed and bound in China

ISBN 978 1 474 74076 0
21 20 19 18 17
10 9 8 7 6 5 4 3 2 1

British Library Cataloguing in Publication Data
A full catalogue record for this book is available from the British Library.

Acknowledgements
We would like to thank the following for permission to reproduce photographs: Alamy: PA Images, 29, roger askew, 23, World History Archive, 5; Getty Images: altrendo images, cover bottom, Ben Pruchnie, 27, Gideon Mendel, 19, Photofusion/Universal Images Group, 17; Shutterstock: Attitude, design element, Elena Rostunova, 15, Ermine, design element, George Rudy, 11, Hannamariah, 21, John Gomez, 9, Lifestyle_Studio, design element, Monkey Business Images, 13, Sarunyu_foto, design element, URRRA, design element, wjarek, 25; Thinkstock: Photos.com, 7

We would like to thank Marguerite Heath, Programmes Director at the Citizenship Foundation, for her invaluable help in the preparation of this book.

Every effort has been made to contact copyright holders of material reproduced in this book. Any omissions will be rectified in subsequent printings if notice is given to the publisher.

All the Internet addresses (URLs) given in this book were valid at the time of going to press. However, due to the dynamic nature of the Internet, some addresses may have changed, or sites may have changed or ceased to exist since publication. While the author and publisher regret any inconvenience this may cause readers, no responsibility for any such changes can be accepted by either the author or the publisher.

Contents

Some words are shown in bold, **like this**. You can find out what they mean by looking in the glossary.

What is individual liberty?

Individual **liberty** means that every one of us has a right to certain **freedoms**. These include freedom of speech and belief, and freedom from violence and fear. Individual liberty is one of four key British values. These values help people to understand how to behave.

Your freedom, my freedom

Individual liberty does not mean doing exactly what we like! It means **respecting** the freedoms of others, too. It can be hard to balance our own **rights** with those of others. Sometimes we think our own needs are the most important. The way we act affects our friends, family, neighbours and people at school or work.

Around the world

In Britain and Northern Ireland, laws and codes uphold individual liberty. Many countries around the world have similar laws. But in some countries, people have little freedom and few rights.

The Task Team investigates

Amina, Emily and Kwame are the Task Team. They report on school and community issues for their class. This time, the Task Team investigates individual liberty through a local incident.

THE
Declaration and Standard

Of the *Levellers* of *England* ;
Delivered in a Speech to his Excellency the Lord Gen.*Fairfax*,
on *Friday* last at White-Hall, by Mr.*Everard*, a late Member of the
Army, and his Prophesie in reference thereunto ; shewing what will
befall the Nobility and Gentry of this Nation, by their submitting to
community ; With their invitation and promise unto the people, and
their proceedings in *Windsor* Park, *Oatlands* Park, and severall other
places ; also, the Examination and confession of the said Mr. *Everard*
before his Excellency, the manner of his deportment with his Hat on,
and his severall speeches and expressions, when he was commanded
to put it off. Together with a List of the severall Regiments of Horse
and Foot that have cast Lots to go for *Ireland*.

Imprinted at *London*, for *G. Laurenson, Aprill 23. 1649.*

Over 350 years ago, this document put forward ideas of individual liberty for England and the world.

YOU *Decide!*

Is individual liberty important to you? See if you change your ideas as you read this book.

Fact FILE

British values mean the values of the United Kingdom of England, Wales, Scotland and Northern Ireland. British laws support individual liberty. From the age of ten, we can be taken to court for breaking laws.

We should all be allowed in!

Not so fast. Upsetting the shopkeeper won't solve ANYTHING!

As your Task Team reporters, we offer to investigate. Maybe we can change the shopkeeper's mind!.

The journey to individual liberty

A thousand years ago, Britain was divided into different kingdoms. Each had its own laws, rights and values. They were created by and for each king and his nobles, not for the poor and powerless.

Then in 1176, King Henry II of England set out some small changes in a document called the Assize of Northampton. For the first time, people without power had a few rights.

Mighty Magna Carta

The Magna Carta of 1215 was a charter, or list of rights. It outlined the first individual freedoms. In it, all people had the right to a fair trial. Even the king had to obey the law. King John I of England (reigned 1199–1216) drew up the charter, under pressure from his angry **barons**. They resented the king's total power.

Fact FILE

Some countries and organizations have adopted ideas set out in Magna Carta. They include:

- The United States, in their Bill of Rights (1791)
- The **United Nations** (see pages 26-27), in their Universal Declaration of Human Rights (1948)
- The European Convention on Human Rights (1950)

Do you think the shopkeeper's stopping our rights, Grandma?

NO! And in my day, we just did as we were told!

The barons renewed their support for King John when he signed the Magna Carta on 19th June 1215.

The first Bill of Rights

By the 1600s, Great Britain as a single nation was taking shape. In 1647, an English political group called the Levellers pressed for individual liberties in a document called "An Agreement of the People". It led to the first official Bill of Rights in 1689.

Many changes were made over the next 300 years. Then, in 1998 a modernised **Human Rights** Act was passed in Parliament. This Act says that everyone in the United Kingdom has the right to be treated equally, with fairness, dignity and respect.

Grandma's just old-fashioned. Let's check on our rights.

Well, if we all go in at once, it looks like the shopkeeper can claim TRESPASS!

Freedom of expression

In Britain, we are all allowed to **express** our ideas and opinions. We can show what we think or feel through speech, writing, music and artwork. This right is one of our most important individual freedoms.

How did freedom of expression happen?

Over 1,000 years ago, kings, queens and other powerful people could express themselves without punishment. The majority of citizens could not do this until the Magna Carta was signed (see page 6). This charter allowed ordinary citizens to speak a little more freely.

Today, Britain follows the freedoms declared in the European Convention of **Human Rights**. This is because Britain has also politically been a part of Europe since 1972. Britain belongs to the **United Nations** (UN), too. This international organisation supports freedom of expression.

Get INVOLVED!

Try to express something important to you. You could do it through drawing, painting, sculpting, poetry or music.

8

Stifling our freedoms

In the past, some rulers stopped people from expressing their religious beliefs. During the 16th and 17th centuries, this especially affected those who wanted to keep their **Catholic** faith. They did not want to follow the national **Protestant** religion.

At this time Catholic artists often included secret **symbols** in their works. These symbols represented the artists' true beliefs.

Article 11 of Britain's Human Rights Act allows peaceful protest in the UK.

Spreading gossip and lies

Should we express our opinions even if they upset someone? Social media and texting can spread hurtful words and images very rapidly. It is very easy to put comments on to social media. But once a comment has been posted on a website it can be difficult to remove it. When we use these media, we should consider how other people will feel when they read our comments. This is an important issue for all of us today.

What's the law?

If people spread lies about us they could be taken to court for **defamation**. This law protects people from having lies told about them. Defamation means trying to destroy a person's good name by spreading lies about them.

One type of defamation is **slander**, when lies are spread through spoken words. The other is **libel**, when lies are spread through written words and visual forms.

Fact FILE

In Britain, personal data and information are protected by:

- **The Human Rights Act, 1998**
- **The Data Protection Act, 1998**

Get INVOLVED!

With friends, draw speech bubbles. Fill each one with expressions you have heard that seem hurtful. Replace the words in bubbles with kinder ways of expressing the point.

Keeping things to ourselves

We can usually trust people we know with personal information. But sometimes, words we speak, or photographs we share, leak out. Information about our private lives can easily fall into the hands of people who do not care about our feelings. This is why there are **privacy** laws to protect us.

But in 2016, the Investigatory Powers Act was passed. Under this Act, British **intelligence** agencies can legally access and keep information taken from our computers and smartphones.

Research finds that young people become isolated and depressed if they use social networking sites too much.

Freedom to meet

In Britain we have the freedom to meet and speak with anyone we choose. It does not matter where they come from, their background, **faith** or ability. We can gather together in groups, both large and small. These rights are called "freedom of association" and "freedom of assembly".

What stops us from mixing?

We are sometimes unsure about speaking to people who are not like us. They might be new neighbours or children in our class. They might be from a different culture, ethnic background or faith from us. Sometimes we feel this way because we hear other people saying bad things about them. But individual **liberty** means that we do not have to agree with those opinions. We have the freedom to make up our own minds.

Safety first!

We meet together at school, clubs, sports grounds, places of worship and often in family gatherings. Sometimes we meet new people when we go on holiday. We should enjoy speaking with others and having fun. But individual liberty allows us to speak up if we feel unsafe with anyone. It also allows us to protect others who we think are in danger.

YOU Decide!

What would help you to speak to someone your age who is different from yourself? Think about things you might share, such as hobbies, TV programmes or fashions.

Fact FILE

The **Terrorism** Act of 2000 investigates and stops organisations that are planning to harm people. It is unlawful for us to belong to them.

The interests, activities and learning that we share are more important than differences in our backgrounds.

If we say you don't meet him, then you DON'T! OKAY?'

See that? That's the school's new CCTV camera. We've been filmed!

Freedom of movement

Individual **liberty** allows us to travel freely around the United Kingdom (UK). This means that we do not need a passport to move between England, Wales, Northern Ireland and Scotland. We can travel freely to the UK's 5,000 tiny islands, too.

Your journeys

Sometimes, adults need to show **identification** to prove they have bought tickets to an event, museum or gallery. This means they need to carry a photo of themselves and details of their name and address. But most of the time, we do not need to prove who we are. In some European countries people all have identification cards. But wherever we go and however we travel, we do have to obey laws on how we behave.

There are some places that we are not allowed to enter. You might see signs that say, "Private Property", "No Entry" or "No Trespassing". This might be because the land is privately owned or unsafe. Our homes or gardens are also private. The law protects them from **trespass**, which means unlawful entry.

YOU Decide!

All around the world, people need passports to travel to other countries. Does a passport **express** our freedom to travel, like buying a ticket? Or is it a way of controlling our movements?

I think it's polite if we take a letter to the shopkeeper.

I'll come with you. But I'll wait outside.

I suppose we should find out the shopkeeper's name.

WHAT? You don't even KNOW?! He's Mr Kaminsky!

In times of conflict

From 1969, high walls and barbed wire divided the **Catholic** and **Protestant** faith communities in Northern Ireland. This is because a minority of people within each community was in **conflict**. These barriers were known as "peace walls". They stopped the free movement of people. Many of them still remain.

Some European Union countries belong to an area called the Schengen zone. People who live there do not need passports to travel within it.

So what do you think of the letter so far?

We could add that only three of us will meet him.

Yes. "Task Team" sounds huge and threatening!

I'll say that an adult is coming. too.

Freedom of religion

In Britain, individual **liberty** means we are free to practise any religion, or no religion. We are also free to change our beliefs. Religions are also known as **faiths**, and Britain is described as a multi-faith society.

Religion and rule

Britain's monarchs (kings and queens) have been linked to Christianity for hundreds of years. Our monarchs must belong to the **Protestant Anglican** church (Church of England), and so do not share the religious freedoms of other people in Britain.

Our national Christian churches are the Church of England and the Church of Scotland. The laws on monarchs and churches were established between 1688 and 1707.

Fact
FILE

British laws on freedom of thought and **faith** are backed by:
- European Union **Human Rights** charter, Article 9.
- **United Nations** Human Rights charter, Article 18.

What does this mean for us?

Since 1707, laws on religious freedom have changed many times. So now, Britain's faiths include other Christian churches, as well as Buddhism, Hinduism, Judaism, Islam and Sikhism, among others.

Each faith has its own codes and ceremonies. These often mark different stages of responsibility in our lives. An example is the Jewish Bar Mitzvah, usually for 13-year-old boys, and Bat Mitzvah for 12-year-old girls. They celebrate a child growing towards adulthood. From this time, the child is responsible for following his or her religious codes.

Sikhs in Britain or any other country adopt the traditional day of worship wherever they settle. In Britain, this is Sunday.

There's no time to meet now. I'll allow you all in the shop for Diwali. But afterwards, I want a meeting. Then, we must both write some RULES!

Thank you, Mr Kaminsky!

We'll try to make sure Diwali goes smoothly.

Expressing our faith every day

The values of each faith are taught in Britain's many places of worship. Ideas and beliefs that are similar to British values lie at the heart of each faith. These include **respect**, **tolerance** and equality towards all individuals.

Dress and faith

Some faiths recommend dress codes for their followers. For many Muslim boys and girls, this means that they should wear **modest** clothing that covers the body well. School uniforms usually allow for these codes. Girls might wear headscarves, and trousers layered with a tunic. Boys might wear long sleeved shirts and loose trousers. Many Sikh boys tie their uncut hair into a knot that is covered with a cloth called a *patka*.

When faith is misused

Individual liberty does not give us the freedom to use our beliefs to harm others. Sometimes, people do not study their faith properly and use it violently. Some people are distorting the values of Islam to support **conflict** in Britain and around the world.

It is not hard to include faiths, fashion and comfort in a school uniform.

Get INVOLVED!

Find out about different faiths in your area. Festivals are a good way to start. You will find that most people are very happy to share their feasts and festivals with everyone. Food codes and recipes are another great way of finding out about faiths and cultures.

Just make sure you keep to your promise!

THANK YOU, MR KAMINSKY!

So now we must meet with Mr Kaminsky, and work out some fair rules. Hmmm.

KENFIELD STORE POST OFFICE

Responsibilities as well as rights

Individual **liberty** does not mean that we are more important than anyone else. We should make sure that other people's **rights** are **respected**, too. This means that we should use kindness and respect when we **express** an opinion.

Other people's feelings

Caring about other people's feelings shows respect for their individual liberty. It shows responsibility when you include a lonely classmate in your conversation. Rejecting vicious gossip about people also shows responsibility, and a lot of strength.

It is easy to follow the crowd, especially if they are your friends. Social media can quickly spread unkindness. But individual liberty gives us the right to choose kindness, too.

Being a good neighbour

Thinking about our neighbours shows respect for their individual liberty. They have a right to live without worry. Some of our neighbours are elderly. Others might be unwell or disabled, or they could be caring for a newborn baby. This means they might become stressed if there is a lot of noise outside their home. We need to consider the needs of our neighbours.

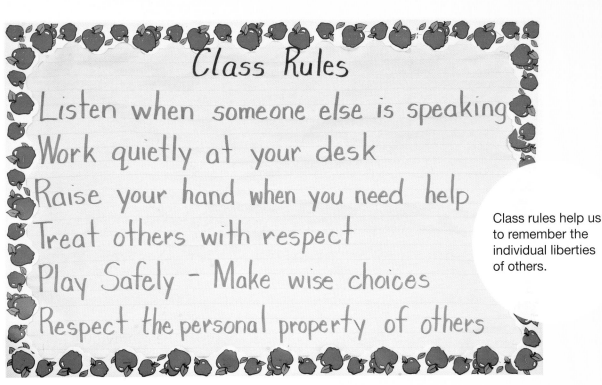

Class Rules

Listen when someone else is speaking

Work quietly at your desk

Raise your hand when you need help

Treat others with respect

Play Safely - Make wise choices

Respect the personal property of others

Class rules help us to remember the individual liberties of others.

Fact FILE

On Safer Internet Day in 2016, a survey showed that over 30 per cent of 10–13-year-olds had seen social media "online hate".

YOU Decide!

Children under 13 should not open social media accounts. Does this stop individual liberty? Should there be more more social media education before children use it?

It says. "Three girls pushed in front of the whole queue."

And. "A boy knocked over an elderly lady!"

That's why I started the two-at-a-time rule. My other customers have the right to be served in peace and safety. I had to do SOMETHING.

Liberties without laws

Some of our **freedoms** involve personal choice, rather than law. Personal choice can be a positive individual **liberty**. But it is sometimes hard to choose well. Other freedoms are supported by laws laid out in the **Human Rights** Act of 1998. But governments sometimes fail to enforce the laws.

The freedom to achieve

Every child in Britain has the freedom to go to school. Here, we can develop our talents through hard work, education and training. But sometimes we find it hard to study. Often we cannot seem to discover what we are best at. This is when we need the help of responsible adults. The **United Nations** (UN) has tried to make sure that support happens with its Rights of the Child charter. Article 29 of this charter is about developing talents through education. But it is hard to enforce this.

The freedom to eat healthily

In Britain, we can choose what we eat. There is no law that tells us what we may or may not eat. Companies that produce our food are free to make whatever sells the best. This can mean producing and selling cheaper foods, which often contain a lot of fat and sugar. These foods have led to a high rate of obesity in Britain. Healthy foods such as vegetables and fruits can be expensive. This means people with little money feel that they do not have the freedom to choose.

It is a right and freedom to live in a warm, dry home with enough space. But by the autumn of 2016, 74,600 men, women and children did not have a proper home. They were living in temporary accommodation.

We are free to make things happen. These children are growing vegetables for a healthy lifestyle.

We've published our Shop Battle story in the Gazette and webpage.

What good will that do?

It shows both sides of the story.

Parents, and other kids can read it and help us work out FAIR rules.

Individual liberty around the world

Each country in the world has its own individual **liberty** laws and practices. They come from the country's own histories and cultures. Britain is seen as having more liberties than some parts of the world.

Different freedoms

Some countries have different ideas about individual liberty. They may be quicker or slower to change laws on individual liberties. Their governments might want to control their citizens' **freedoms**.

Other countries do not support laws on individual liberty very well. This might be because they do not have enough police officers and lawyers to investigate broken laws. It might be because a government does not want its citizens to move freely or to be free to set up political organisations. This type of government is often afraid of losing its power.

Poverty and individual liberty

When a country becomes poorer, individual liberties sometimes suffer. This also happens where there are a few rich people and a lot of poor people. In these countries, a government fears that poverty will lead to unrest among its people. So people's **rights** are reduced in order to control them.

Fact FILE

- About 40 per cent of the world's population has a high level of individual freedom.
- About 24 per cent has partial freedom.
- About 36 per cent has little freedom.

YOU Decide!

Do you think we should trade with or give aid to countries that have few individual liberties? Do you think we should keep talking to them? If we stop talking, how can we **express** our ideas about individual liberty?

Demonstrations against government control of the public media took place in Poland in 2016.

Liberty and the United Nations

The **United Nations** (UN) is an international organization that was formed in 1945, after World War II. Its aims are to keep peace in the world and to defend **human rights**. These rights include individual liberty.

Thirty rights for all

The UN has not been able to stop a lot of wars. But it tries to make its member countries follow the UN Universal Declaration of Human Rights, drawn up in 1948. This is a list of 30 rights and freedoms that we should all enjoy.

The Declaration is translated into 500 different languages, so most people around the world can understand their rights under international law. One of the most important rights is given in Article 3 of the Declaration. This states that we all have the right to life, liberty and security.

Special rights for children

The United Nations Rights of the Child is a charter of 54 important Articles that outline children's liberties. Article 28 supports a child's right to education, while Article 29 supports the development of talents. It is hard to enforce Article 29, as we saw on page 22. Article 31 **expresses** the right to rest and play!

Universal Children's Day is celebrated on 20th November each year to mark the Declaration of the Rights of the Child.

Fact FILE

- There were 193 member countries of the UN in 2017.
- The countries of Kosovo, Taiwan and Vatican City in Italy are not yet members.

The future for individual liberty in Britain

Do we have enough individual **freedom**, or too much? Do we balance our **rights** and responsibilities? So, do we give as well as take? These are things to think about all our lives. But what is the future of individual **liberty** in Britain?

New relationships – new laws

Britain has its own laws on individual liberty. These included freedom of movement and the right to live and work in the European Union (EU). But Britain voted to leave the EU in 2016.

It will take a long time to cut links fully with the EU and work out our freedoms within it. Whatever the choices, Britain will still belong to the European Court of **Human Rights**, which includes European countries outside the EU.

YOU Decide!

- Should there be a Youth Parliament to put forward ideas on individual liberty?
- Should individual liberties be increased by allowing 16-year-olds to vote in elections?

We've made one, too!

I've made a Charter of Rights – for you AND me!

Our charters look almost the same!

AMAZING!

Individual liberty for all

It is tempting to think only about our own rights. But Britain has a long tradition of supporting individual liberty around the world. We see **refugees** fleeing from war. Or they may be fleeing from **persecution** because of their political beliefs, **faith** or culture.

The UN Human Rights Article 14 supports refugees' rights to seek asylum (safety) in another country. Will Britain take this into consideration in the way it treats refugees seeking to live here?

Britain's Youth Parliament allows young people aged 11-18 to debate values and laws.

Glossary

Anglican relating to the Church of England

baron nobleman in medieval times

Catholic relating to the Roman Catholic church; the religion followed in Britain until the 16th century

conflict violent disagreement

defamation trying to destroy someone's good reputation by spreading lies about them

express show how you feel or think by doing something

faith system of religious belief

freedom state of being free; right to live in the way you want

human rights basic rights to be treated fairly, that everyone in the world should have

identification something that proves who a person is

intelligence information secretly gathered by spies or electronic devices

libel false statements that are written or printed

liberty freedom from restriction or control

modest decent, not showy

persecution cruel or unfair treatment often because of race or religious beliefs

privacy state in which others do not disturb or interfere with your personal matters

Protestant relating to the branch of Christianity that broke off from the Catholic church in the 16th century

refugee person forced to flee his or her home because of natural disaster or war

respect accept that someone has certain rights

rights legal or moral entitlements

slander false statements that are spoken

symbol sign that stands for something

terrorism use of violence and destructive acts to create fear and to achieve a political or religious goal

tolerance acceptance of people's beliefs or actions that differ from our own beliefs or actions

trespass entering someone else's property without permission

United Nations (UN) international organization formed to keep peace in the world and to defend human rights

Find out more

Books

You might like to look at these other books on British Values:

It's the Law! (British Values), Christopher Yeates (Gresham Books, 2016)

Looking After Britain (British Values), Christopher Yeates
(Gresham Books, 2016)

What Does It Mean to be British?, Nick Hunter (Raintree, 2017)

Websites

www.bbc.co.uk/newsround
The CBBC Newsround website gives lots of interesting features on rights and values around the world.

www.un.org/en/universal-declaration-human-rights/
On this site you can read the United Nations Declaration of Human Rights.

www.unicef.org/rightsite/files/uncrcchilldfriendlylanguage.pdf
Read the UNICEF Rights of the Child at this site.

Index